THE BIG BOOK OF

DINOSAURS

A First Book for Young Children

To Jeremy with Love
Granddad Christmas '94.

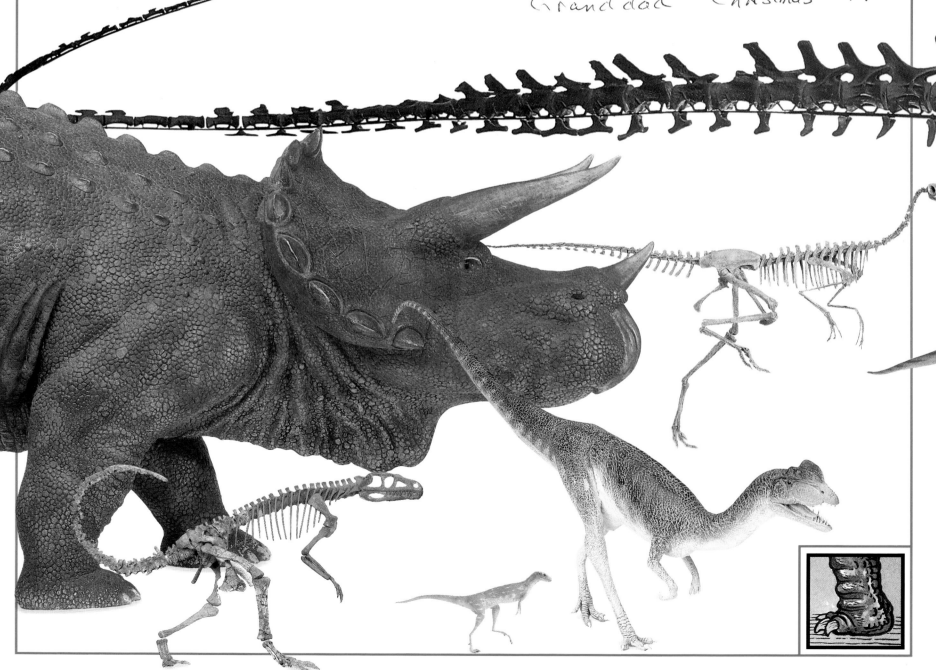

A DORLING KINDERSLEY BOOK

Editor Lara Tankel Holtz
Designer Mary Sandberg
Production Louise Barratt
Illustrator Dorian Spencer Davies
Consultant William Lindsay

First published in Great Britain in 1994 by Dorling Kindersley Limited,
9 Henrietta Street, London WC2E 8PS

Published in Canada in 1994 by Scholastic Canada Ltd.,
123 Newkirk Road, Richmond Hill, Ontario L4C 3G5

Canadian Cataloguing in Publication Data

Wilkes, Angela
The big book of dinosaurs

Includes index.
ISBN 0-590-24371-3

1. Dinosaurs - Juvenile literature. I. Title.

QE862.D5W5 1994   j567.9'1   C94-931538-9

Color reproduction by Pica Overseas Ltd.
Printed and bound in Italy by Mondadori

THE BIG BOOK OF
DINOSAURS

A First Book for Young Children

Angela Wilkes

Scholastic Canada Ltd.

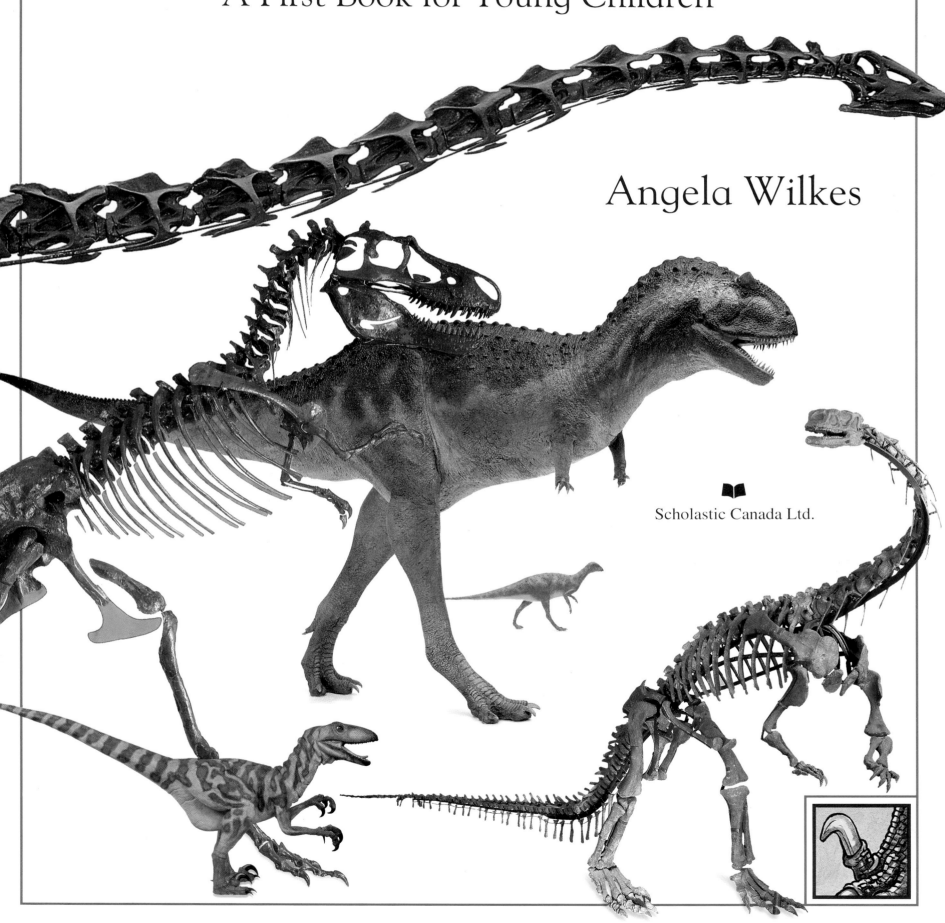

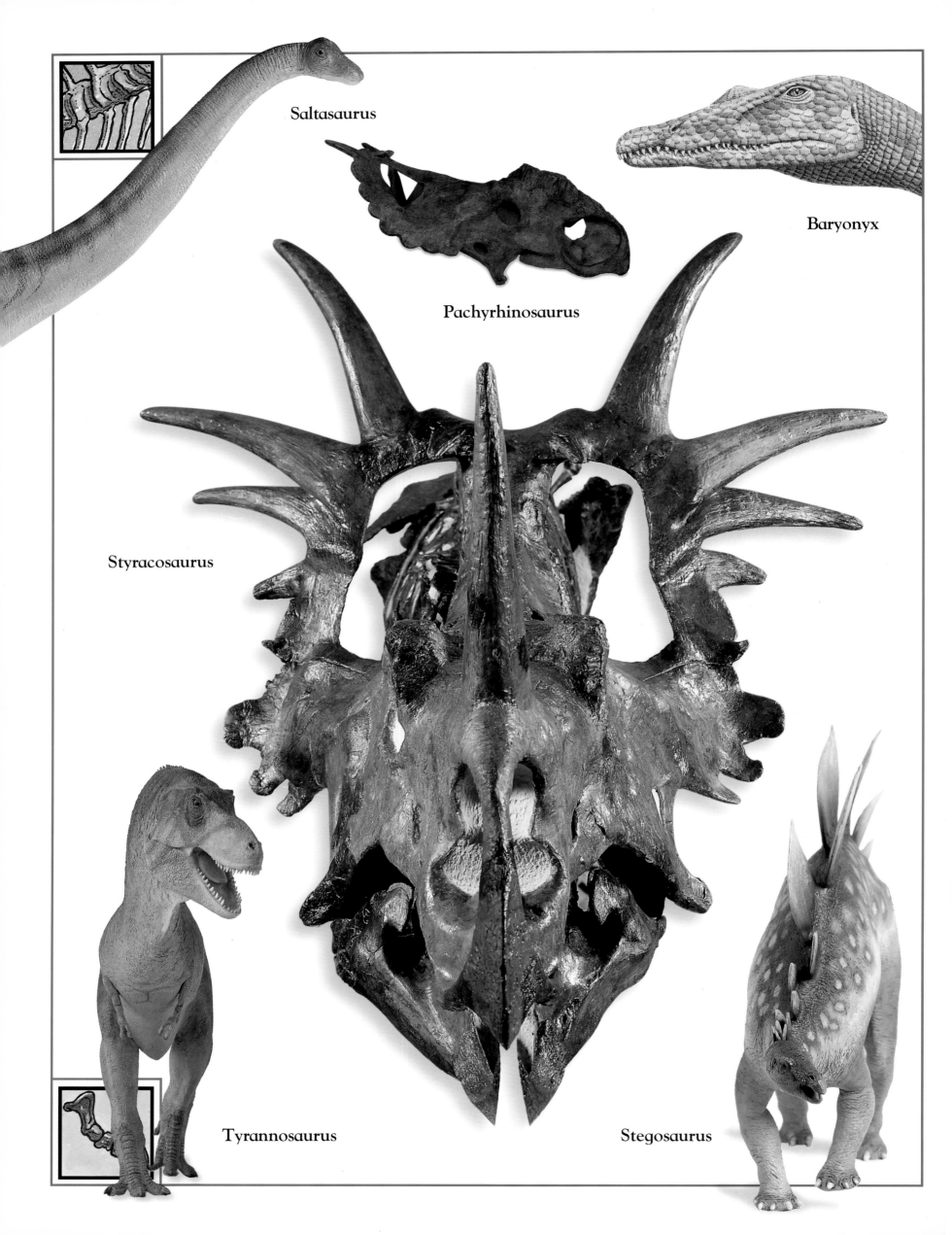

Saltasaurus

Baryonyx

Pachyrhinosaurus

Styracosaurus

Tyrannosaurus

Stegosaurus

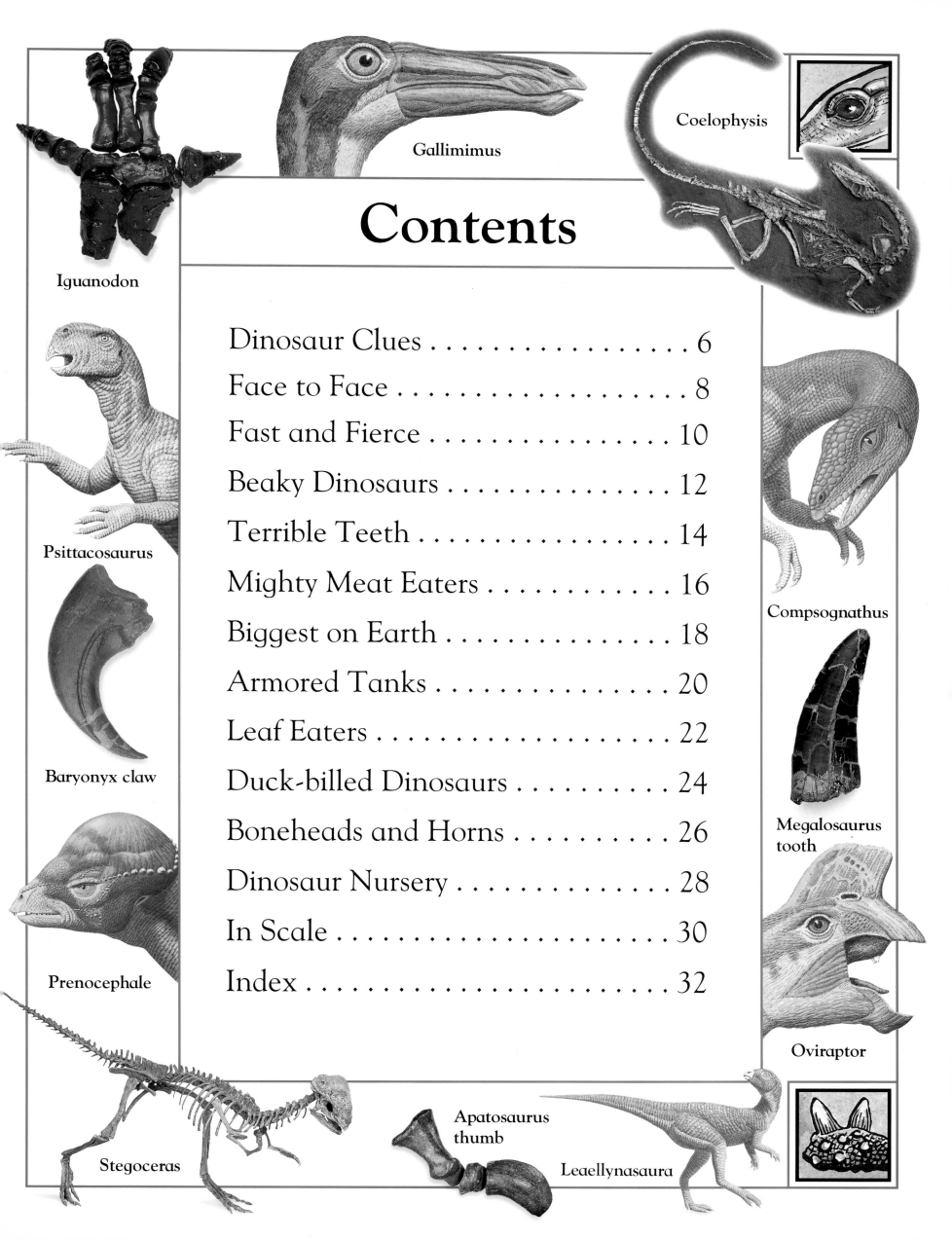

Iguanodon

Gallimimus

Coelophysis

Contents

Psittacosaurus

Baryonyx claw

Prenocephale

Compsognathus

Megalosaurus tooth

Oviraptor

Stegoceras

Apatosaurus thumb

Leaellynasaura

Dinosaur Clues

This hole shows where the dinosaur's eye was.

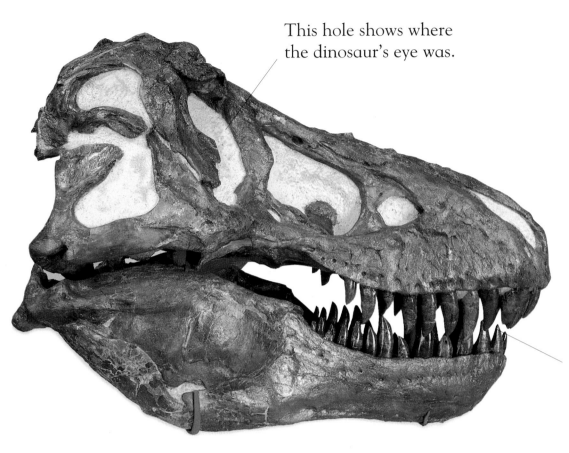

Tyrannosaurus skull

Clues to the past

How do we know so much about dinosaurs when the last one died millions and millions of years ago? Scientists hunt for the fossil remains of dinosaur bones and teeth buried in rocks. They use these as clues to figure out as much as they can about dinosaurs.

Tyrannosaurus's huge jaws and teeth show that it was a fierce meat eater.

Rebuilding a dinosaur

Scientists can fit a dinosaur's fossil bones back together to build a whole skeleton. They can make models of any bones that are missing.

Heavy tail helps balance its body.

tail bones

foot bone

heavy claws

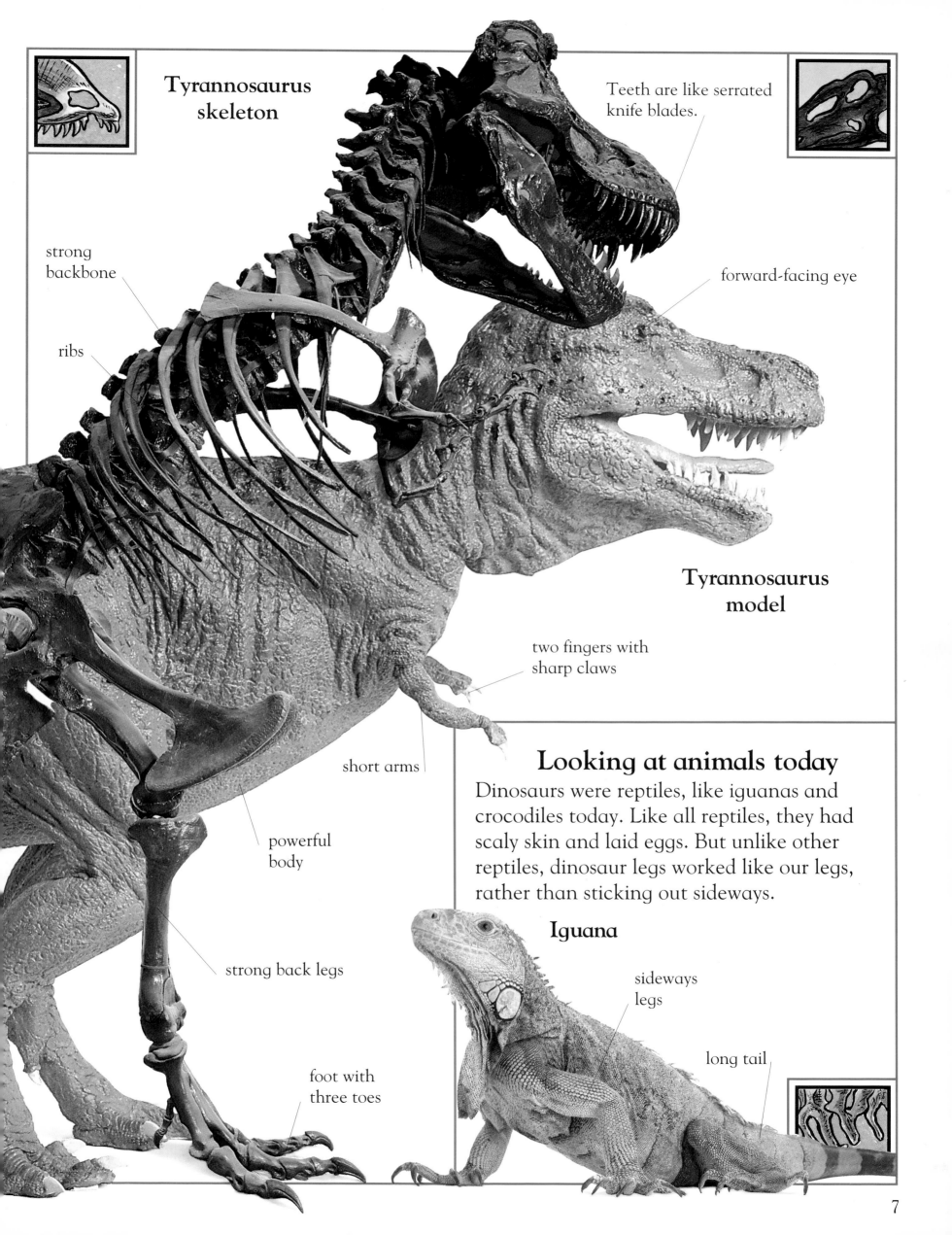

Tyrannosaurus skeleton

Teeth are like serrated knife blades.

strong backbone

ribs

forward-facing eye

Tyrannosaurus model

two fingers with sharp claws

short arms

powerful body

Looking at animals today

Dinosaurs were reptiles, like iguanas and crocodiles today. Like all reptiles, they had scaly skin and laid eggs. But unlike other reptiles, dinosaur legs worked like our legs, rather than sticking out sideways.

Iguana

strong back legs

sideways legs

long tail

foot with three toes

Face to Face

Portrait gallery

The dinosaurs shown on this page are all different shapes and sizes. Some had spikes to defend themselves, some had bony lumps for protection, some had many sharp teeth, but others had no teeth at all.

Euoplocephalus

Euoplocephalus was an armored dinosaur, covered in bony lumps and bumps.

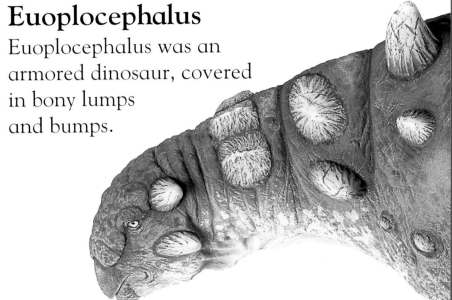

Corythosaurus

This duck-billed dinosaur had a head crest like a plate standing on edge!

Triceratops

This big plant eater had a head frill and three sharp horns.

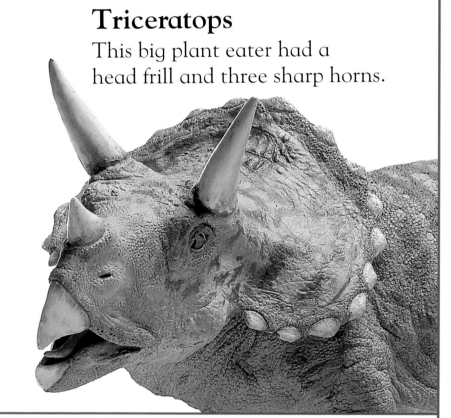

Stegosaurus

This plant eater had two rows of plates down its back.

Oviraptor

Two-legged Oviraptor was a hunter with a strange beak and a crest on its head.

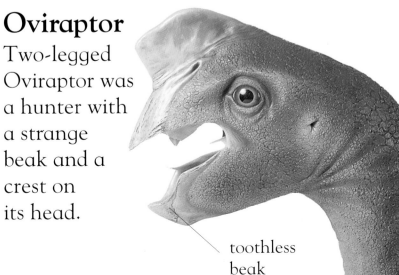

toothless beak

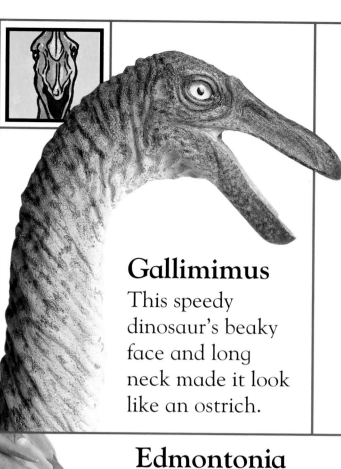

Gallimimus

This speedy dinosaur's beaky face and long neck made it look like an ostrich.

Compsognathus

Fierce and tiny Compsognathus was no bigger than a chicken.

Lesothosaurus

This small dinosaur was an agile runner.

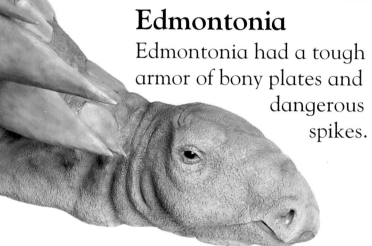

Edmontonia

Edmontonia had a tough armor of bony plates and dangerous spikes.

Iguanodon

Iguanodon was a big, plant-eating dinosaur with many strong teeth and spiked thumbs.

Pachycephalosaurus

This dinosaur had a domed, bony head that looked like a crash helmet.

Barosaurus

This gigantic plant eater's neck was more than 30 feet (9m) long.

Fast and Fierce

Deinonychus

Deinonychus was a fast and very fierce dinosaur. It attacked its prey by slashing out with the long, curved claws on its feet. It also had razor-sharp teeth for tearing off chunks of flesh.

Troodon's large eyes faced forward.

Troodon

This quick-witted dinosaur had a very big brain. Its large eyes helped it hunt for prey at night.

Deinonychus had 70 jagged teeth for eating tough prey.

These fearsome claws were as long as a whole human hand.

Deinonychus used this sharp claw to slash its victims.

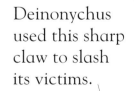

Dromaeosaurus

This skull shows that Dromaeosaurus had powerful jaws lined with saw-edged teeth.

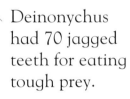

Ornitholestes

Ornitholestes was light and speedy with a very long tail. It probably hunted small reptiles.

Herrerasaurus used its long tail to help it balance.

Herrerasaurus

Herrerasaurus was one of the first dinosaurs, living 225 million years ago. It was as big as a small car and armed with sharp teeth and claws.

What do you think Herrerasaurus used its strong, curved claws for?

Its narrow head is like a bird's.

Compsognathus

Tiny Compsognathus lived 150 million years ago. It could run very fast to catch small lizards and insects to eat, gripping them between its hands.

Its long legs and feet helped it run fast.

Beaky Dinosaurs

large beak

Ornithomimus

Ornithomimus was a toothless, birdlike dinosaur. It had a small head, a long, thin neck, and a beak. It had very powerful back legs. Can you guess why?

big toes with claws

Struthiomimus

Like Gallimimus, Struthiomimus was an "ostrich" dinosaur, but it had no feathers.

Inside its beak there were small, sharp teeth.

Archaeopteryx

Archaeopteryx is the oldest bird known. It had teeth and a tail like a reptile, but it also had feathers like a bird.

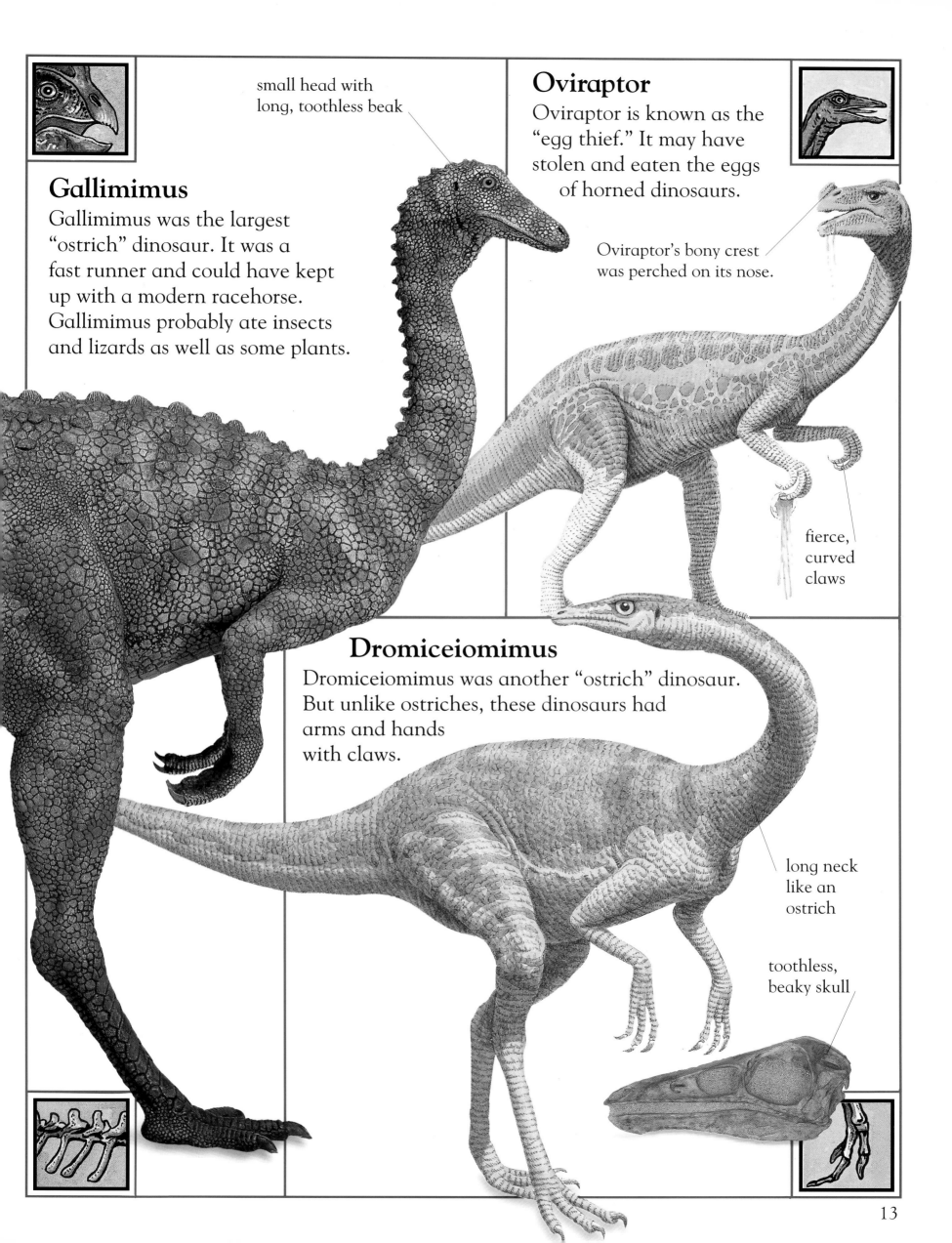

small head with
long, toothless beak

Oviraptor

Oviraptor is known as the
"egg thief." It may have
stolen and eaten the eggs
of horned dinosaurs.

Oviraptor's bony crest
was perched on its nose.

Gallimimus

Gallimimus was the largest
"ostrich" dinosaur. It was a
fast runner and could have kept
up with a modern racehorse.
Gallimimus probably ate insects
and lizards as well as some plants.

fierce,
curved
claws

Dromiceiomimus

Dromiceiomimus was another "ostrich" dinosaur.
But unlike ostriches, these dinosaurs had
arms and hands
with claws.

long neck
like an
ostrich

toothless,
beaky skull

Terrible Teeth

Tyrannosaurus

Scientists can tell what kind of food an animal eats by looking at its teeth. Tyrannosaurus had huge jaws, lined with long, saw-edged teeth, that could open very wide. What do you think it ate?

Megalosaurus

Megalosaurus's teeth were like curved daggers. When a tooth broke or wore out, a new one grew in its place.

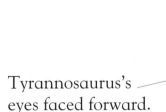

Tyrannosaurus's eyes faced forward. This helped it judge distances when attacking prey.

fossilized Megalosaurus tooth

These jaws were strong enough to crush bones.

Tyrannosaurus's teeth were as long as table knives.

Allosaurus

Allosaurus was a savage meat eater. Its teeth were sharp and saw-edged for slicing through flesh. They curved backward to give Allosaurus a firm grip on its victims.

serrated, bladelike teeth

Diplodocus

Diplodocus was an enormous plant eater. It had thin teeth, like small pencils, used for raking up leaves and ferns.

Diplodocus only had teeth at the front of its mouth.

Compsognathus

This little meat eater had sharp eyes for searching out prey to crunch between its sharp teeth.

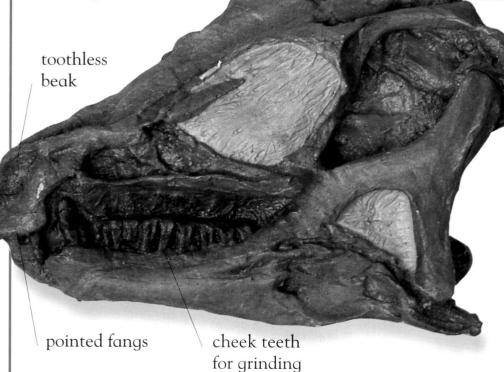

toothless beak

pointed fangs

cheek teeth for grinding

Heterodontosaurus

Heterodontosaurus was an unusual plant eater. It had a horny beak and three kinds of teeth for cutting and grinding.

15

Mighty Meat Eaters

Carnotaurus's head looked like a bull's head.

Carnotaurus

The fiercest dinosaurs were the two-legged meat eaters such as this Carnotaurus. It had a big head, strong legs, and short arms. It hunted other dinosaurs or ate dead animals that it found.

Dilophosaurus

Dilophosaurus means "two-ridge lizard." It gets its name from the two crests on its head, which look like two plates standing on edge.

Allosaurus

Allosaurus lived in North America 150 million years ago. It attacked and ate big plant eaters such as Diplodocus.

Ceratosaurus

Ceratosaurus had a short, thick neck, a huge head, and a bony horn on its snout.

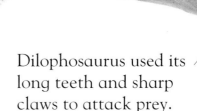

Dilophosaurus used its long teeth and sharp claws to attack prey.

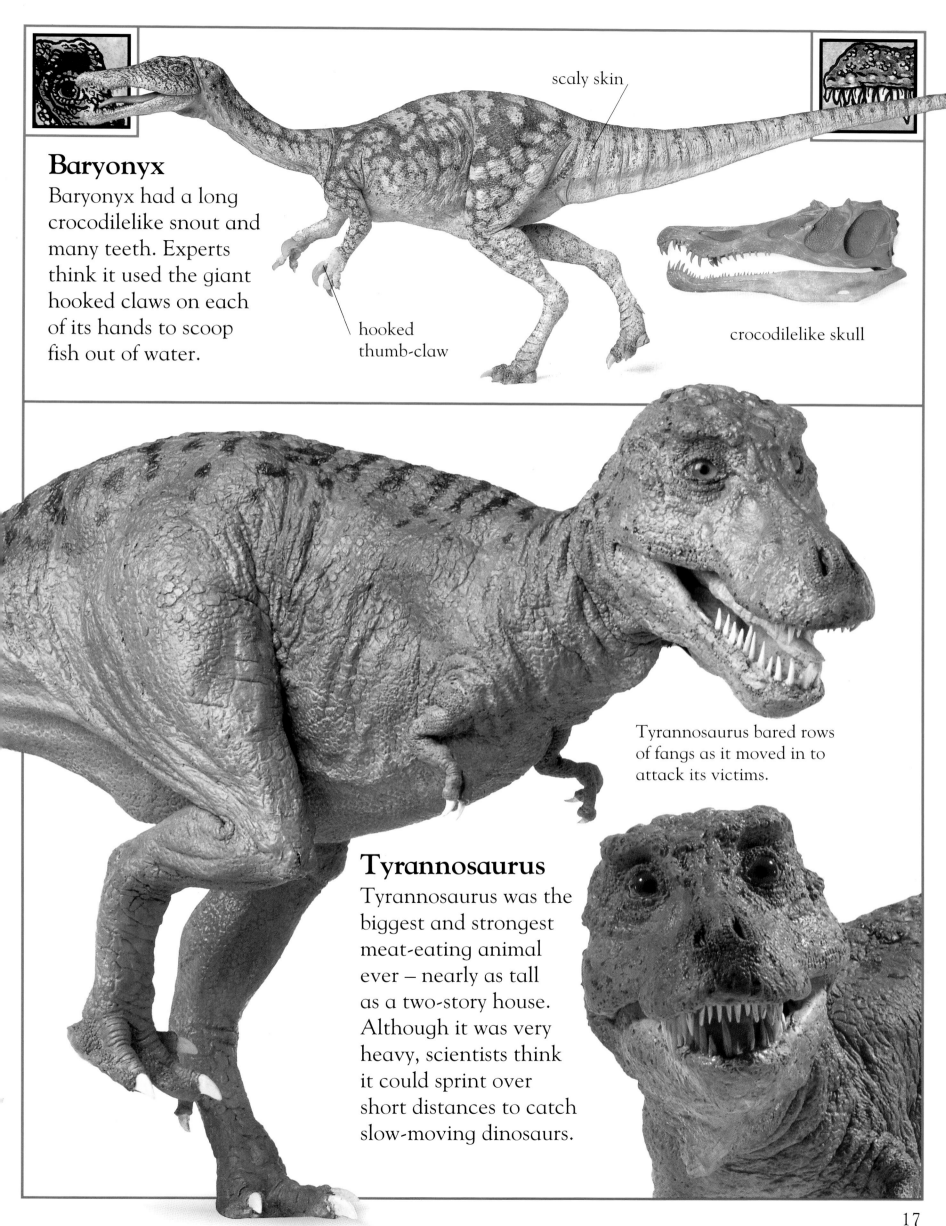

Baryonyx

Baryonyx had a long crocodilelike snout and many teeth. Experts think it used the giant hooked claws on each of its hands to scoop fish out of water.

scaly skin

hooked thumb-claw

crocodilelike skull

Tyrannosaurus bared rows of fangs as it moved in to attack its victims.

Tyrannosaurus

Tyrannosaurus was the biggest and strongest meat-eating animal ever – nearly as tall as a two-story house. Although it was very heavy, scientists think it could sprint over short distances to catch slow-moving dinosaurs.

Biggest on Earth

Apatosaurus

Apatosaurus had short, sharp teeth for gathering leaves from plants. This dinosaur was so big, it probably spent most of its day eating.

Mamenchisaurus

Mamenchisaurus had the longest neck of any animal ever – 50 feet (15m) long. That's three times as long as a giraffe's neck!

Its long, thin tail was carried off the ground.

Lufengosaurus

This skeleton of Lufengosaurus is standing on its back legs.

Diplodocus

Diplodocus looked like a walking suspension bridge. It was longer than a tennis court! Despite its massive size, it only had a tiny brain.

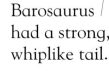

Barosaurus had a strong, whiplike tail.

Plateosaurus

Plateosaurus was always looking for food to fill its big, bulky body.

Saltasaurus

Saltasaurus's back and sides were protected by bony, pea-size lumps beneath its skin.

Can you guess why Saltasaurus needed armor-plating?

long, sloping neck

Barosaurus

Barosaurus was the tallest of the dinosaurs. It could reach treetops as high as a five-story building. Because of its height, some experts think it had eight hearts!

Barosaurus's heavy neck was held up by strong, ribbed bones.

Armored Tanks

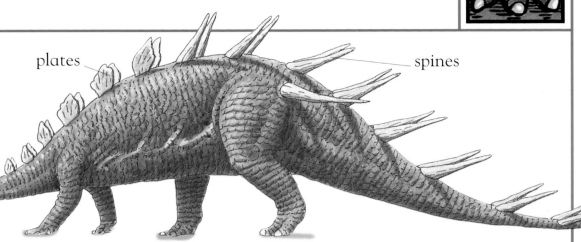

Kentrosaurus

Kentrosaurus was a slow-moving plant eater. It had bony plates and spines along its back. The pairs of spines above its back legs helped protect it from attackers.

plates

spines

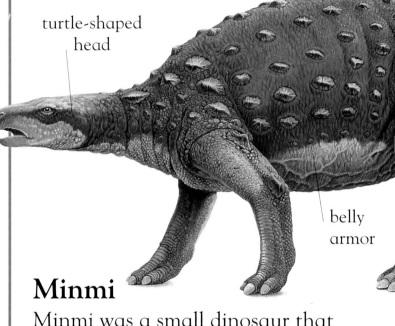

turtle-shaped head

belly armor

Minmi

Minmi was a small dinosaur that lived in Australia. It was so well protected that it had bony plates on its belly as well as its back.

Experts think that the bony plates along Stegosaurus's neck and back helped keep it cool in hot weather and warm in cold weather.

Stegosaurus

Stegosaurus was the largest of the plated dinosaurs. It ambled slowly along, munching on plants. Stegosaurus probably used its fierce spiked tail as a club when defending itself from hungry meat eaters.

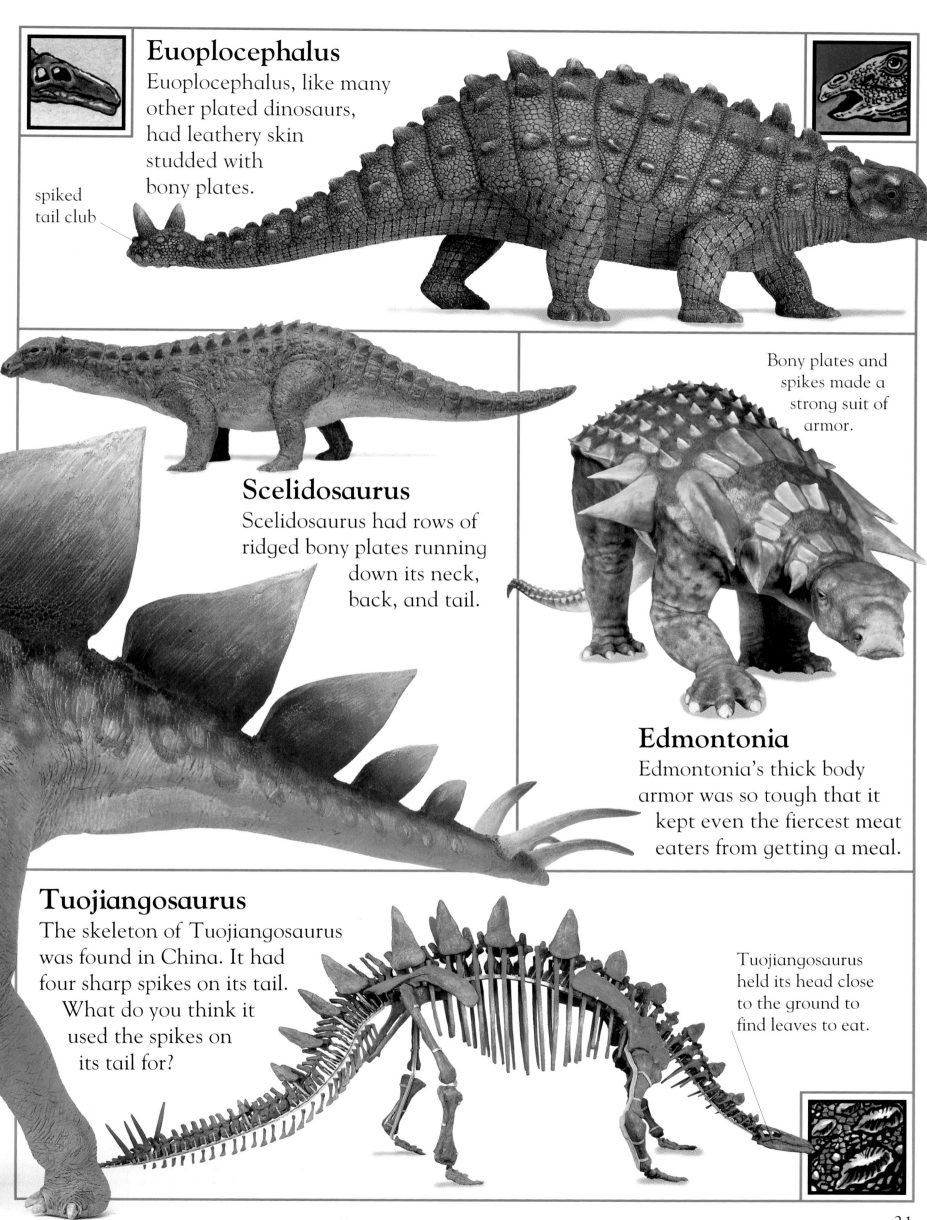

Euoplocephalus

Euoplocephalus, like many other plated dinosaurs, had leathery skin studded with bony plates.

spiked tail club

Scelidosaurus

Scelidosaurus had rows of ridged bony plates running down its neck, back, and tail.

Bony plates and spikes made a strong suit of armor.

Edmontonia

Edmontonia's thick body armor was so tough that it kept even the fiercest meat eaters from getting a meal.

Tuojiangosaurus

The skeleton of Tuojiangosaurus was found in China. It had four sharp spikes on its tail. What do you think it used the spikes on its tail for?

Tuojiangosaurus held its head close to the ground to find leaves to eat.

Leaf Eaters

Lesothosaurus

Lesothosaurus was a tiny dinosaur, not much bigger than a dog. It looked like a lizard standing up on its back legs.

Heterodontosaurus may have used its hands to dig in the sand for roots or to tear open insect nests.

Heterodontosaurus

Heterodontosaurus was small and probably ate leaves and roots. It could run very fast to escape from hungry meat-eating dinosaurs.

three long toes on each foot

Hypsilophodon

Hypsilophodon was a speedy dinosaur. It grazed in herds because this was safer than roaming alone.

long toes with sharp claws

The front of Iguanodon's mouth was shaped like a beak.

Iguanodon

One of the best-known dinosaurs, Iguanodon, was much bigger than many other leaf eaters. It could probably walk on two legs as well as on all fours.

Iguanodon had strange spiked thumbs. It may have used them to defend itself.

Iguanodon's tail balanced its large body.

Hypsilophodon's long legs show that it was a fast runner.

Duck-billed Dinosaurs

Edmontosaurus had powerful jaws and hundreds of teeth for chewing tough leaves.

Saurolophus

Saurolophus had a flap of skin between its beak and crest. Scientists think the dinosaur used this to make loud honking calls.

Parasaurolophus's long crest was hollow inside.

Parasaurolophus

For a long time, experts thought Parasaurolophus's crest was used to help it breathe. Now they think it helped make the dinosaur's calls louder.

Edmontosaurus

Edmontosaurus wandered around in slow-moving herds. Like the other duck-billed dinosaurs, it ate plants.

Shantungosaurus

Shantungosaurus was probably the biggest duck-billed dinosaur.

hatchet-
shaped
crest

bony,
hollow
crest

Lambeosaurus

Lambeosaurus had a beak like a
duck. It also had a hollow crest
shaped like a hatchet.

Corythosaurus

Corythosaurus means "helmet
lizard." It had a thin, flat
crest on its head. Scientists
think these crests helped
the dinosaurs recognize
one another.

The bony crest
formed part of
the skull.

Corythosaurus had
long fingers and
short claws.

Boneheads and Horns

Styracosaurus

Styracosaurus was one of many horned dinosaurs. It had a head frill with sharp spikes.

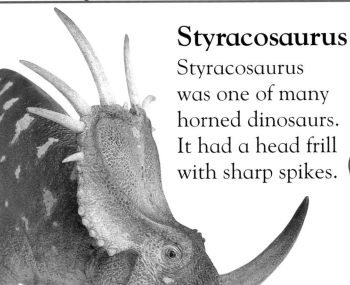

Psittacosaurus

This early dinosaur was called Psittacosaurus, or "parrot reptile," because it had a beak like a parrot's.

Stegoceras

Stegoceras had a bony, egg-shaped head. Its stiff, heavy tail helped balance the weight of its body.

Triceratops

Triceratops was like a huge rhinoceros with a massive three-horned head. As it munched on plants, it used its fearsome horns to defend itself against meat eaters.

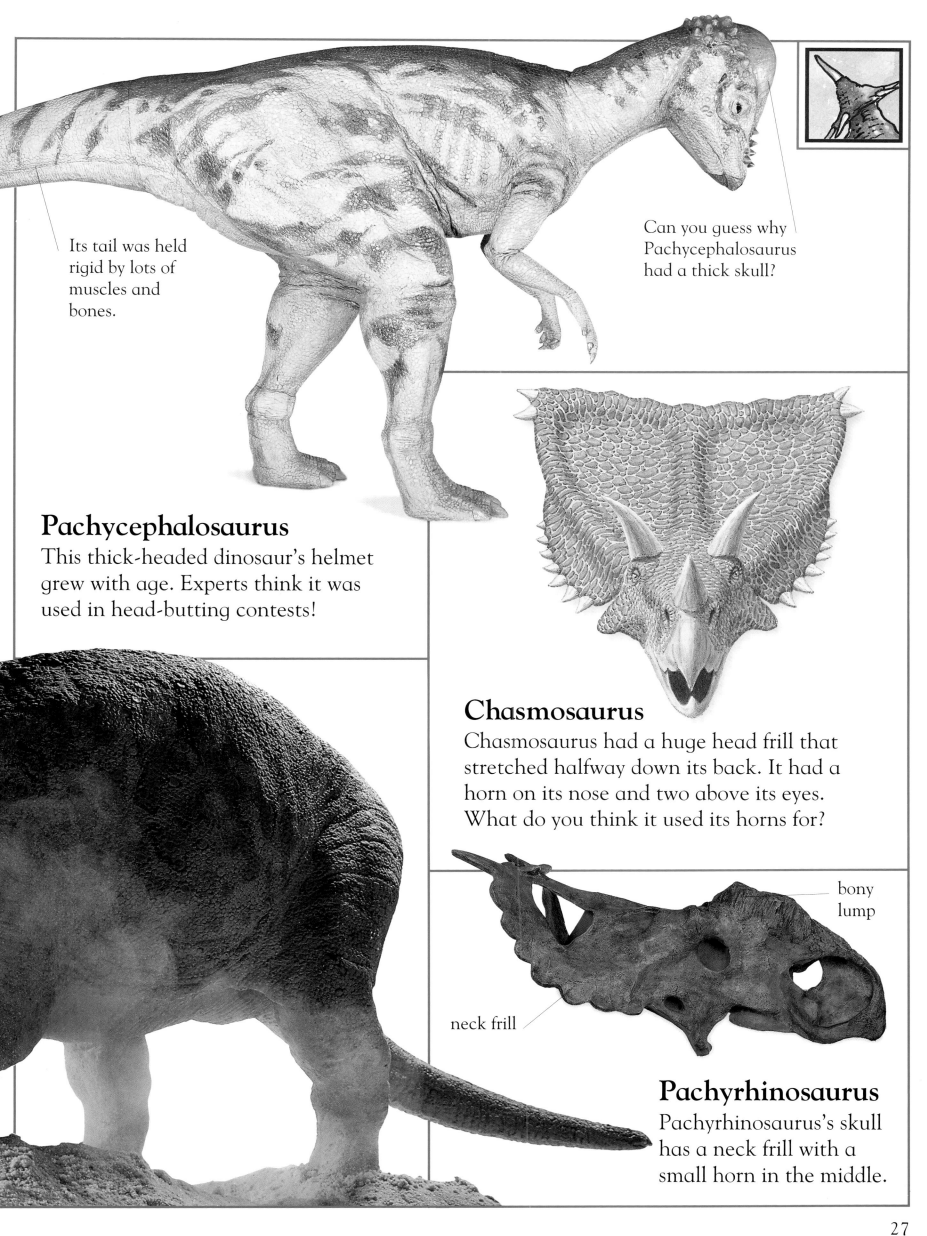

Its tail was held rigid by lots of muscles and bones.

Can you guess why Pachycephalosaurus had a thick skull?

Pachycephalosaurus

This thick-headed dinosaur's helmet grew with age. Experts think it was used in head-butting contests!

Chasmosaurus

Chasmosaurus had a huge head frill that stretched halfway down its back. It had a horn on its nose and two above its eyes. What do you think it used its horns for?

bony lump

neck frill

Pachyrhinosaurus

Pachyrhinosaurus's skull has a neck frill with a small horn in the middle.

Dinosaur Nursery

This female dinosaur would have looked after a large group of dinosaur eggs.

Orodromeus
This model shows Orodromeus's babies hatching. Fossil eggs of this small, two-legged plant eater have been found in North America.

Nesting together
Dinosaurs laid eggs, like reptiles and birds. Scientists have found fossils of eggs, nests, and babies belonging to duck-billed dinosaurs called Maiasaura. Groups of female dinosaurs built their nests together and looked after the babies once they had hatched.

The nests were mounds of earth hollowed out in the middle.

Protoceratops

Protoceratops laid eggs that looked like big potatoes. They were laid in circles in hollows in the sand.

The babies were about 8 in. (20 cm) long when they hatched.

adult Protoceratops skull

baby Protoceratops skull

Protecting the young

Fossil footprints of the big plant eaters show that they traveled in herds. The adults protected their young like elephants do today.

Why do you think this young Diplodocus stayed close to an adult?

Maiasaura's eggs were pear-shaped and about the size of a human head.

In Scale

From big to little

Many people think that all dinosaurs were huge, but in fact they came in all shapes and sizes, from the gigantic Barosaurus to the tiny Compsognathus.

Did you spot any of these dinosaurs earlier in the book?

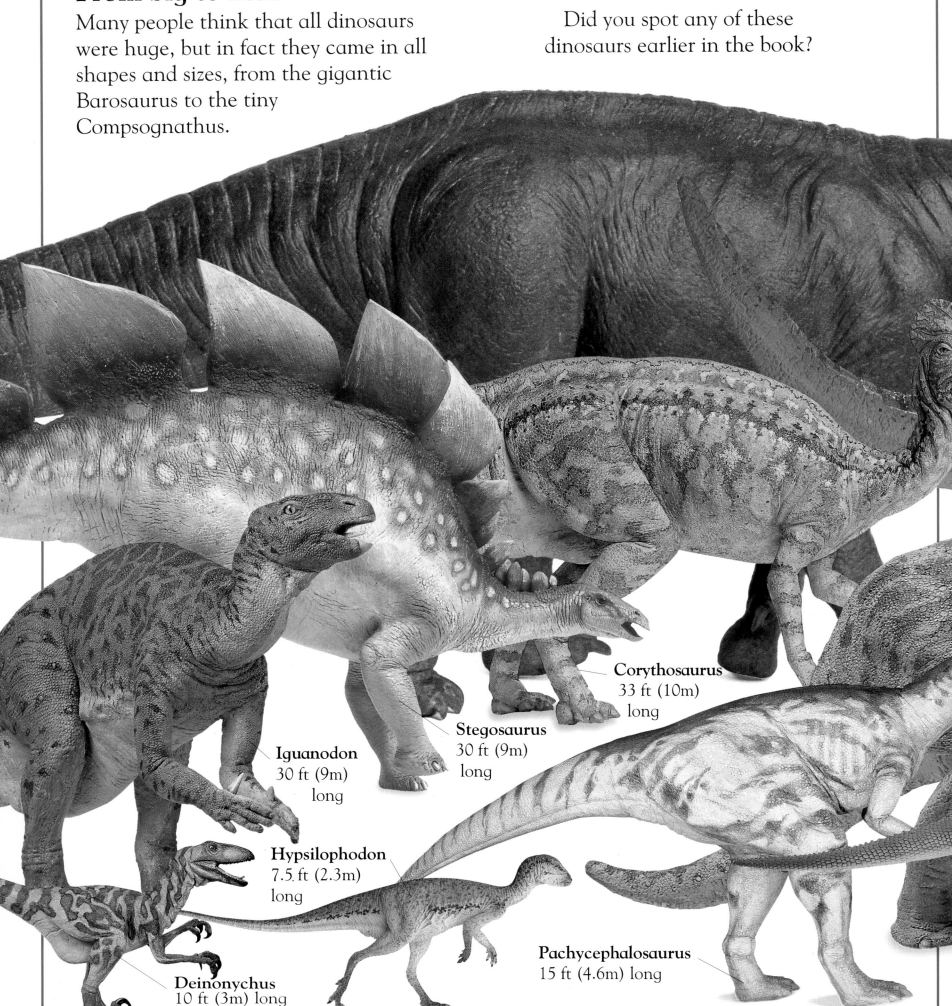

Corythosaurus
33 ft (10m) long

Stegosaurus
30 ft (9m) long

Iguanodon
30 ft (9m) long

Hypsilophodon
7.5 ft (2.3m) long

Pachycephalosaurus
15 ft (4.6m) long

Deinonychus
10 ft (3m) long

Barosaurus
75-88 ft (23–27m) long

Tyrannosaurus
40 ft (12m) long

Euoplocephalus
23 ft (7m) long

Compsognathus
2 ft (70cm) long

Triceratops
30 ft (9m) long

Gallimimus
20 ft (6m) long

Index